LONE STAR SHADOWS
ECHOES *of the* FORGOTTEN

TERESA NORDHEIM

AMERICA THROUGH TIME®
An imprint of SUTTON PUBLISHING INC.
www.through-time.com

First published 2025
Copyright © Teresa Nordheim 2025

ISBN 978-1-63499-555-9

All rights reserved. No part of this publication may be reproduced, stored in a retrieval system or transmitted in any form or by any means, electronic, mechanical, photocopying, recording or otherwise, without prior permission in writing from Sutton Publishing Inc.

Typeset in 10pt on 13pt Sabon
Printed and bound in England

Contents

Introduction — 5

1. Battlefields — 9
2. Marine Corps — 25
3. Navy — 31
4. Army — 48
5. Coast Guard — 62
6. Air Force — 76
7. Space Force — 93

Introduction

From humble beginnings in 1823, the Texas military quickly became a powerhouse. This evolution resulted from the shifting priorities of a growing frontier society.

Military leaders sent troops into the rugged, uncharted lands to protect settlers and negotiate with Indigenous Americans. Their presence sparked clashes with Karankawa, Comanche, and Cherokee tribes. This delicate balance between protection and diplomacy shaped the expanding landscape.

A spark of rebellion flared at Gonzales, Texas, in October 1835. Within weeks, determined Texans rallied to arms, forging dual military branches. The army mustered its ranks on land and appointed Sam Houston as commander in chief. At sea, the navy readied its fleet under the command of Captain Charles Hawkins. Though untried, troops stood poised to fight for Texas's dream of independence.

Established on August 5, 1836, the Texas Military Department unified all state military forces under one banner. The Office of the Adjutant General acted as the human resources department. The army protected the land, while the navy protected the water.

On January 14, 1836, the Texas Navy created the Texas Marines as a naval infantry unit to boost its fighting power. Sharpshooters and boarding experts, these sailors enforced discipline across maritime domains. At sea, they maintained order on ships. Ashore, they secured stations. Their adaptability shone in critical operations, from peacekeeping to tactical assaults.

On September 5, 1836, Texas faced a decisive challenge: defending its newfound independence. The solution? Restructuring the military department again. The Constitution's military article addressed the need for advancement. It created a three-pronged structure. The first and second units, the army and navy, continued their vital roles in land and sea warfare. The third unit included the Texas Army National Guard, Air National Guard, and State Guard.

Texas joined the Union on December 29, 1845, becoming the twenty-eighth state. The Texas Army and Navy merged with the United States Armed Forces on February 19, 1846. Unification brought progress to a growing society, but it meant abandoning bases in Texas.

As bases and battlefields grew silent, people began to talk about lingering spirits, and haunting tales. Soldiers and civilians began to share stories of haunted battlefields and barracks that go bump in the night.

The Texas Military Forces Museum displays retired equipment and vehicles allowing the public to see these mighty machines up close. (*Articseahorse*)

Anti-aircraft guns have been around since 1949 and continue to assist the army. (*Articseahorse*)

Introduction

Texas recognized the importance of women in the armed forces at an early stage of development. (*Michael Barera*)

A row of massive combat-ready tanks line up at the Texas Military Forces Museum. (*Pi3.124*)

Armor Row at the Artillery Park holds some of the largest museum displays. (*Pi3.124*)

Here is an example of a plane flown by the Texas Air Guard. (*Pi3.124*)

1
Battlefields

As the battle ends, the chaos of war gives way to an eerie stillness. In Texas, each conflict imprinted freedom more profoundly into the state's soul. Yet, the scars of conflict linger, etched in the ground and buildings that bore witness to it all.

Six flags wave over Texas, resonating with centuries of struggle. They embody the Texan spirit—a relentless pursuit of liberty. Each phase not only marked territorial claims but also shaped the identity of Texans.

1519–1543: Spanish explorers arrived in Texas, seeking new territories for Spain. The Spanish fostered ties with Indigenous Americans. Additionally, explorers recorded their discoveries, crafting maps and reports that shaped future colonization.

1684–1689: France briefly claimed Texas. French explorer René-Robert Cavelier aimed to expand French land rights. The French suffered a series of unfortunate events that contributed to their loss of leadership. This included shipwrecks, disease, famine, and, in the end, the death of their leader.

1690–1821: Spain was eager to keep its top position in the Americas. However, as Mexico sought to expand its influence, tensions escalated, setting the stage for conflict.

1821–1836: Mexican settlers journeyed northward, boldly facing the wild terrain of Texas's frontier. Their arrival created a unique blend of cultures, merging traditions and lifestyles. Tensions rose when Mexican General Santa Anna declared himself dictator.

1836–1845: Texas forged its independence from rebellion to republic through blood and fire. The Texas Revolution ignited in 1835, pitting Texas settlers against Mexican rule. Bexar fell, the Alamo's defenders perished but hope endured. Sam Houston rallied the army, crushing Mexican forces at San Jacinto in 1836. Texas secured the victory and declared itself a sovereign nation.

1845–1860: Texas joined the Union in 1845, becoming America's twenty-eighth state. This annexation expanded U.S. territory and heightened tensions over slavery's westward spread.

Long after the cannon fire, the historic grounds of the battlefield remain restless. (*25or6to4*)

This painting depicts the Texas Revolution and the historic fight at the Alamo. (*Welcome2sunshine*)

Battlefields

Memorial signs mark the history of abandoned fields. (*Carol M. Highsmith*)

As nature reclaims the battlefields, it can be difficult to envision the battles and the bloodshed. (*Carol M. Highsmith*)

Above: Painting such as this show the terror and mayhem which the citizens of Texas faced while fighting for their independence. (*Henry Arthur McArdle*)

Left: Monuments mark the victory and honor of the Texas Revolution. (*Jim Evans*)

1861–1865: During the Civil War, the Confederacy controlled Texas. It used its resources and strategic position to maintain this control, which persisted until Texas rejoined the Union in 1865.

Paranormal experts agree that hauntings often stem from tragic, sudden deaths. The sad histories of battlefields spark speculation about the supernatural, leading many to believe that the past still haunts us. This enlightens a world of possible ghosts in the abandoned buildings in Texas.

Fort Defiance: Presidio La Bahía

In 1747, the Spanish Army built Presidio La Bahía in Goliad, Texas, to defend against possible threats. Despite construction challenges and staff shortages, the fort became a key site.

The Texas Revolution began in Gonzales on October 2, 1835, when Texas declared war on Mexico. The second skirmish began at dawn on October 10, 1835. The Texas Army wanted to capture Mexican General Martín Perfecto de Cos. Stationed at Presidio La Bahía, the Mexican soldiers organized a robust defense. The Texans, aided by Goliad's citizens with axes, managed to breach the fort.

Moments after the lone watchman's warning, troops fatally wounded the guard. About thirty minutes of shellfire erupted before the Mexican Army surrendered. Texans boldly proclaimed their victory and renamed the site Fort Defiance.

On March 2, 1836, officials signed the Texas Declaration of Independence at the fort. A momentous occasion that continues to evoke reverence as the birth of the Republic of Texas.

The Mexican Army regained control of the fort on March 27, 1836. Over 450 Texans found themselves prisoners at Fort Defiance. The sick and injured rested in the chapel. Unaware of their impending fate, over 400 able-bodied Texans lined up in the fort. Mexican forces opened fire at point-blank range. Those Texans who survived the rampage of bullets met their doom with clubs and knives. Those in the chapel met their deaths as well.

When silence returned to the fort, only twenty-eight Texans remained alive. The fort, once a symbol of resistance, now bore witness to one of the nation's deadliest massacres in the state.

This darkness lingers, and visitors hear distant cries, screams, gunshots, and cannon fire. People feel unseen eyes upon them as they walk the battlefield. When night falls, an eerie presence envelops these hallowed grounds as invisible soldiers walk the battlefield.

The officers' quarters are open to overnight visitors brave enough to endure the challenge. According to reports, the beds are comfortable. However, the overwhelming feeling of doom makes it nearly impossible to sleep.

The spirits at Fort Defiance linger, filled with rage, pain, and haunting fury. The memories of long-ago conflicts remain, etched into the very soil. The spirits of fallen warriors forever haunt these war-torn lands.

The rugged remains of Fort Defiance shine in the summer sun. (*Ken Lund*)

The fortress is marked with the six flags which flew over Texas. (*Ken Lund*)

In the background, the bell and the cross demonstrate the beauty of the chapel inside the historic fort. (*Ken Lund*)

From Spanish rule to joining the United States, Texas can be viewed through the flags representing each country which claimed leadership of the state. (*Ken Lund*)

The peaceful exterior hides the torment and loss of life which took place in these walls. (*Ken Lund*)

Barred windows and strong wooden doors closed the entrance to the fort. (*Ken Lund*)

Battlefields

Today Fort Defiance is a tourist attraction and a reminder of the fight for freedom. (*Ken Lund*)

While Texas could hide its past, the state wears its flags like a badge of honor. (*Ken Lund*)

The entrance to Goliad State Park and historic site is welcoming. (*Larry D. Moore*)

Another monument to honor those who fought in the war and lost their lives attempt to be independent. (*P6150*)

The Alamo

Spanish Franciscans founded Mission San Antonio de Valero in 1718 to spread Christianity among Indigenous Americans. Ironically, the site's peaceful origins contrast sharply with its eventual fate. The mission hosted Texas's most infamous battle, etching its name in the history books. In 1793, the mission became secularized, leading to its abandonment.

In 1803, the Alamo Company, a cavalry company, occupied the mission for more than ten years, which is why people call it the Alamo.

The mission served as a political prison during the Mexican War of Independence and housed San Antonio's first hospital from 1806 to 1812. Almost ten years later, General Martín Perfecto de Cos captured the Alamo, passing from Spanish to Mexican control.

In December 1835, the Texas Army conquered the mission, and after Cos's departure, many believed the war was over.

February 23, 1836, over 2,000 Mexican troops set forth to reclaim the Alamo. With merely 200 soldiers, the Texan Army could do little to repel the attack.

On March 6, 1836, the Mexican Army launched a fierce assault on the Alamo. This pivotal confrontation marked a significant moment in the Texas Revolution. The battle's toll was devastating. Reports indicated that at least sixty Mexican soldiers lost their lives. On the Texan side, the death count soared to over 250. The brutal conflict lasted for nearly two weeks, culminating in this tragic event.

Hauntings began mere days after the final bloodshed, transforming the site from a place of defeat to a supernatural triumph against mortal intruders. Mexican General Andrade sent a team to burn down the Alamo chapel, but spectral guardians had other plans. The initial squad fled, unnerved by soldiers wielding flaming swords at the entrance. Determined, Andrade led a second expedition. This time, a tall male spirit materialized on the roof, sending the general and his men into a hasty retreat.

Authorities ordered the mission's demolition, sparing only the chapel and barracks. Centuries-old walls pulsed. Spirits stirred, emerging from slumber. Ghost inhabitants saw their home's impending fate.

Visitors often report seeing a fair-haired young boy on the rooftop just after sunrise. As the image of the boy distorts, a man appears and holds the boy in his arms. Many believe it is the perpetual image of a father holding his dying son.

A solitary figure drifts silently along the outer walls, his weary posture hinting at an eternal watch over the grounds. A Mexican soldier, his posture conveys weariness. Hands clasped behind his back, chin dipped low, he wanders the mission grounds.

Ghostly sightings and disembodied voices appear throughout the Alamo, and unseen footsteps haunt its corridors. The museum's atmosphere stirs deep emotions. Guests often leave in tears, overwhelmed by an inexplicable sadness. It blurs the line between sympathy for fallen heroes and supernatural encounters. They leave visitors to ponder the source of their profound experiences.

This painting of the battle at the Alamo proves no one was safe during the heat of the battles which took place. (*Robert Jenkins Onderdonk*)

Once a stone structure that housed those wanting to spread the word of Christianity, the building took on a different purpose. (*Daniel Schwen*)

Tombstones mark just a few of the lives taken during the battle at the Alamo. (*Library of Congress*)

Massive pillars line the front of the history building. (*Speil*)

Highly detailed artwork is sketched into the store entrances and walkways. (*MARELBU*)

Today the Alamo attracts people from all over the world. (*MARELBU*)

Despite years of weather damage and historic battles, the stone buildings remain intact. (*MARELBU*)

A large water fountain adorns the exterior of the building. (*MARELBU*)

Above: This monument holds the names and carved likenesses of several key people in the battle of the Alamo. (*Batlise*)

Left: Metal bars cover the aging glass and keep unwanted visitors from destroying the historical property. (*Jules Verne Times Two*)

2
Marine Corps

The Marine Corps materialized on November 10, 1775, during the Revolutionary War. This new branch tackled ship-to-ship combat, naval discipline, and amphibious operations. Its baptism by fire came against the Barbary pirates in 1801, marking the beginning of a long legacy of service.

The Marine Corps values honor, courage, and commitment. They uphold the highest ethical and moral standards. The corps shows courage through its mental, moral, and physical strength. It demonstrates its commitment with unwavering dedication and a determination to achieve excellence.

Most U.S. states lack active Marine Corps bases; instead, they host numerous reserve centers and often share naval installations.

The operations at Eagle Mountain Lake exemplified these values, where the corps trained its aviators to embody honor and courage in the skies.

The Marines make their tanks strong, sturdy and loaded with weapons. (*Lance Corporal Lukas Kalinauskas*)

Dressed in their formal attire, Marines showcase their desire to have everything neat and orderly. (U.S. Embassy Ghana)

Target practice takes place daily to ensure Marines are in top form and ready for battle. (*Lance Corporal Samantha L. Jones*)

Trucks such as this one allow the military to transport their massive weapons to various locations. (*Fritzmann2002*)

Marine Corps Air Station Eagle Mountain Lake

In 1942, the U.S. Marine Corps acquired 2,931 acres of land and built a training base along Eagle Mountain Lake. The base trained pilots in the techniques of flying gliders during combat. Toward the end of World War II, the base served as a finishing school for dive bombers headed to the South Pacific.

On June 30, 1943, officials designated the base a naval air station. This decision marked the end of the brief, six-month Marine Corps glider program. Many mourned this change even as testing of remote-control planes continued unabated. Engineers refined designs and capabilities year after year. In 1944, a pivotal decision uprooted operations, and the company relocated the entire program to Michigan.

On April 1, 1944, the Marines regained control of the base. In December, the sleepy base was abuzz with activity as it welcomed Marine Aircraft Group 53, a pioneering unit specializing in night fighter operations. This marked a significant milestone, as MAG-53 became the first night fighter group to call the base home. The roar of aircraft engines starting, the bright runway lights cutting through the darkness, and the buzz of activity in the hangars all marked the start of a new era in military aviation. As the Marine Corps' elite aviators converged on the base, the quiet fields hummed with F4U Corsairs and F6F Hellcats. Their sleek silhouettes showcased the cutting-edge technology of the time.

On October 7, 1970, a fighter jet exploded in flight over the area. Witnesses watched as the jet started to glow like a meteor and then burst into small pieces, killing the two crew members on board.

Once bustling with activity, by 1973, the base stood silent, a forgotten relic of the past. While the base doesn't seem to have ghosts, the abandoned base is haunting.

The lake at Eagle Mountain is perfect for fishing and boating activities. (*Gordon Reid*)

Photos from space show the size of the lake and former military base. (*Johnson Space Center*)

Another view from space shows the rest of the area. (*Johnson Space Center*)

While Marines often find themselves housed next to other branches of the military, they are always ready to join in the battle as a team. (*Corporal Juan Torres*)

3
Navy

Faced with the formidable threat of British warships, the fledgling U.S. government recognized the urgent need for a naval force and founded the navy on October 13, 1775.

The navy must be combat-ready to protect American waterways and ensure freedom of navigation and commerce. Navy subs glide through dark waters, vigilantly monitoring, silently gathering intelligence, and acting as a deterrent to potential threats. These hidden guardians safeguard nations, carrying out crucial clandestine tasks. The navy also excels in humanitarian efforts, providing critical disaster relief and medical services.

The navy has three core values: honor, courage, and commitment. These values shape interactions with troops, superiors, and civilians. They guide actions and relationships from combat zones to civilian roles.

As far as the abandoned vessels and bases, once bustling with activity, they now whisper tales of the past. Unseen forces seem to linger.

While the U.S. Navy primarily works to protect the waterways, they are still trained to fight on land. (*Mass Communication Specialist 3rd Class Blake Midnight*)

The navy is shown here watching over *Air Force One*. (*Cherue A. Thurby*)

Above: Navy SEALS are a special unit which requires a diverse set of skills. (*U.S. Navy SEALS*)

Right: Navy men and women are at home on boats and in the water. (*U.S. Navy Serviceman*)

USS *Texas*

One of the navy's notable vessels, the USS *Texas*, played a significant role in both world wars.

As tensions simmered, President Wilson deployed the freshly commissioned USS *Texas* to Mexican waters in March of 1914. Wilson's gambit paid off, and the USS *Texas* completed its first mission without a hitch. This show of strength successfully deterred potential attacks.

During World War I, the ship served as a guardian of the North Sea within the Grand Fleet. The USS *Texas* made history by firing the first American shots of the war.

Extensive renovations and repairs during the war kept the USS *Texas* operational. The upgrades improved its weapons and crew quarters, boosting combat readiness and comfort.

World War II allowed the USS *Texas* to join the Neutrality Patrol to prevent conflict from entering the Western Hemisphere.

On October 23, 1942, the USS *Texas* joined its first major combat. This marked a shift from patrol to active warfare. The ship became a formidable force in critical naval battles, showcasing its devastating firepower and unmatched resilience.

Sometimes Navy SEALS are launched from airplanes into diving locations. (*U.S. Navy SEALS*)

Shown here is a U.S. Army boat which most likely holds several navy men and women too. (*Photographer's Mate 1st Class Shawn Eklund*)

A large crowd gathered to watch the launch of the USS *Texas* on May 18, 1912. (*Library of Congress*)

Operation Torch, the invasion of North Africa, started as a peaceful mission. It turned into amphibious warfare, and no one knew how to proceed. The U.S. Army requested the USS *Texas* to fire on the French Army. Walter Cronkite, then a budding journalist, reported from the USS *Texas*. This would foreshadow his future as a leading voice in American journalism.

The USS *Texas* joined the fleet on D-Day, unleashing a barrage of 255 shells in just over half an hour. Its rapid-fire cannons roared at 7.5 rounds per minute. The next day brought grim reminders of the war's toll: thirty-five injured, one fatally wounded. The ship's role in history's bloodiest invasion was further etched by the arrival of a fallen Coast Guardsman and twenty-seven POWs.

During its service, the USS *Texas* experienced only one crew member fatality. During a combat mission in World War II, Helmsman Christen Christensen was at the wheel on the bridge. A German shell hit the armored conning tower beneath the bridge, fatally striking the nineteen-year-old.

Whispers and faint chatter haunt the corridors of a once-seafaring giant. Now anchored in Houston as a museum, this ship holds mysterious secrets. Visitors stroll the ship's weathered decks. They strain to hear whispers of the past and the creaking timbers that echo with every footstep. Strange sounds lurk in every shadowy corner, turning a naval relic into an eerie time capsule. Supernatural, vaporous shapes materialize throughout the vessel. Sudden temperature drops catch the attention of many guests.

A red-headed sailor, often spotted in an outdated uniform, embodies the spirit of camaraderie among sailors. He offers a comforting smile to visitors as he roams the ship's deck and climbs the ladders. Colorized photos of Christen Christensen, who may still be on duty, show reddish hair.

The USS *Texas* now allows visitors to explore the ship. (*Rennett Stowe*)

USS *Texas* deck is beginning to decay despite continuous renovations. (*Gronowski26*)

A view of the barber shop aboard the USS *Texas*. (*Eric Friedebach*)

The mighty guns atop the battleship. (*Roy Luck*)

A comfy night sleep in the bunks of the USS *Texas*. (*Eric Friedebach*)

When under renovation, the USS *Texas* was brought into dry dock for repairs. (*Flightoffancy*)

USS *Lexington*

The original USS *Lexington*, crafted twenty years prior, met its fate in battle in May 1941. The aircraft carrier sank beneath the Coral Sea.

On July 15, 1941, the USS *Cabot*, a new aircraft carrier, emerged from the same shipyard. The shipyard drafted a letter to the navy requesting a formal name change to honor the USS *Lexington*. The naval secretary, Frank Knox, agreed, and the formal name change occurred on June 16, 1942.

The USS *Lexington*'s journey began on September 23, 1942. Her launch marked a crucial step. Yet months passed, and winter arrived before her call to duty. On February 17, 1943, the navy commissioned the USS *Lexington* for wartime service.

The ship sailed to the Caribbean for its voyage and training. During this cruise, the aircraft carrier suffered its first casualty. Nile Kinnick, the celebrated 1939 Heisman Trophy winner and a beloved figure in American sports, flew training flights on the deck. Ensign Kinnick's plane developed a severe oil leak in the air, preventing a safe return to the ship. The plane crashed about 4 miles away. Authorities failed to recover the aircraft or Kinnick's body.

Pearl Harbor welcomed the USS *Lexington* in August 1943. As World War II raged, the mighty vessel joined the fray. Within days, this powerful warrior made a critical attack. By the end of this mission, the ship had brought down twenty-nine enemy aircraft.

In December 1943, the USS *Lexington* sailed to raid Kwajalein. It destroyed one vessel and damaged at least two others. The crew managed to take down over thirty enemy aircraft before a torpedo struck and killed nine people on board. After undergoing necessary repairs, the ship returned to battle.

On November 5, 1944, a Japanese kamikaze pilot crashed his plane into the USS *Lexington*. He intended to cause an immense explosion of flames and did. Fifty U.S. Navy sailors died. More than 152 people sustained severe injuries. A Japanese flag now hangs over the fatal area as a grim reminder.

In total, the USS *Lexington* saw around thirty-four battles. The crew shot down 387 planes in the air and 635 jets on the ground, and around 370 people died on the ship due to war, accidents, and illness. A moving propeller fatally struck one chief petty officer. A female onboard electrician suffered a fatal electrocution. Yes, female. The USS *Lexington* welcomed women sailors aboard, paving the way for their presence at sea.

As the USS *Lexington*'s legacy grew, so did the tales of the spirits that lingered aboard.

The Paranormal Files investigated the USS *Lexington*, which they found docked in Corpus Christi, Texas, on April 25, 2022. They called it one of the most haunted sites in America.

As the investigative crew began, their batteries died. This could indicate ghosts utilizing the energy to manifest. Also, it was challenging to navigate the dark ship with cameras and flashlights.

An unseen presence met the crew during the investigation, bringing hot flashes and nausea. A haunting melody filled the air from a small music box, seemingly playing on its own, sending shivers down the investigators' spines. Despite the pranks, no malevolence lurked aboard. The spectral sailor's advances, while unwelcome, seemed harmless. Inexplicable experiences aside, the atmosphere remained benign.

Today the USS *Texas* stays docked and invites visitors aboard to experience the historic battleship. (*Michael Barera*)

From a distance the battleship looks like a small fishing boat but looks can be deceiving. (*Michael Barera*)

The USS *Lexington* is an aircraft carrier which is currently docked and used as a historical museum. (*Matthew T. Rader*)

The museum is open for visitors to tour the ship inside and out. (*Leonard J. DeFrancisci*)

Standing several stories high, the USS *Lexington* is overwhelming to explore. (*Articseahorse*)

The decks of the USS *Lexington* invite visitors to explore history. (*Larry D. Moore*)

A Japanese flag, covered in markings details some of the tragic history of the ship. (*Articseahorse*)

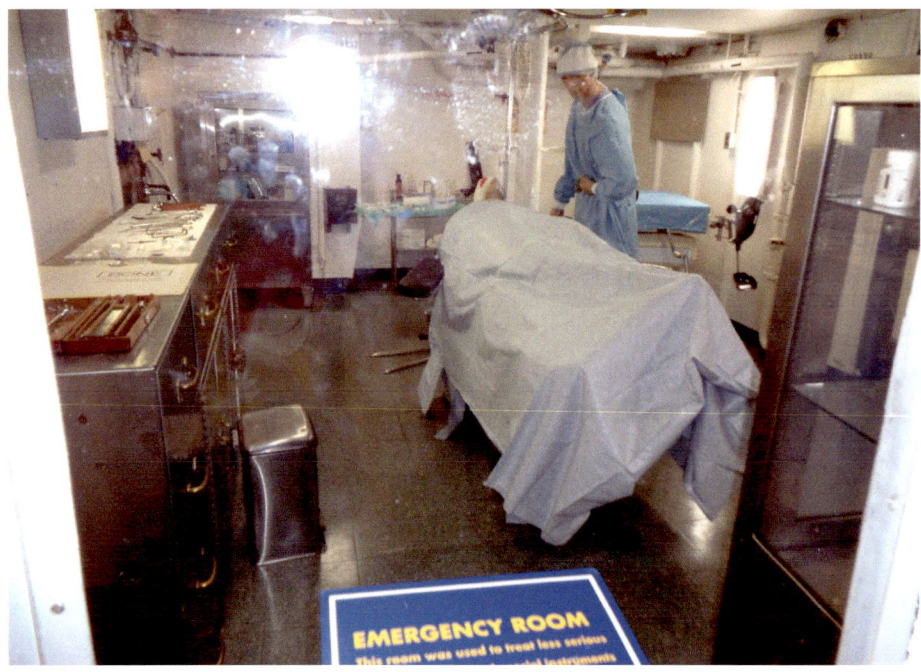
Aboard the USS *Lexington*, the emergency room treated men and women who needed medical care. (*Articseahorse*)

The flag marks the location of the kamikaze plane attack on the ship. (*Articseahorse*)

Several planes are featured on the deck of the USS *Lexington* to show visitors an array of navy planes. (*Articseahorse*)

One area of the ship held sailors for discipline. They slept on small mats that provided little comfort. They weren't allowed to speak and only ate bread and water. In this area, the investigators asked ghosts to turn on and off flashlights. The ghosts complied with light signals and sounds. The ghosts appeared on unique cameras that tracked temperature and movement.

Paul Coffey's team ventured deeper. A ghostly figure in a navy blue uniform locked eyes with them and vanished through a sealed hatch. Undeterred, they pressed on, encountering spirits eager to engage.

Visitors report eerie encounters aboard the haunted ship. Shadow figures dart across the decks, and phantom voices and the sounds of soldiers at work ring out. Museum staff witness unexplained phenomena. Volunteers talk about "the angry chief," a stern spirit patrolling the flight deck. This ghostly officer, once a strict disciplinarian, scowls at passersby. While full apparitions seldom appear, the vessel swarms with activity. When night descends, unseen sailors seem to resume their duties.

Blending pivotal naval history with eerie legends, the USS *Lexington* is a haunting enigma in the water.

Shown here is the F-4A Phantom II fighter jet. (*Articseahorse*)

The large deck of the aircraft carrier is prominent in this photo. (*Alan Wilson*)

4
Army

In 1775, the Continental Army's call drew in eager recruits from the thirteen colonies. By June 14, a unified force stood ready. Under George Washington's leadership, this new army embodied the young nation's resolve. They prepared to fight for freedom.

The army is the land defender and conducts ongoing training to achieve combat readiness. Additionally, it plays a crucial role in humanitarian aid and disaster relief efforts. Peacekeepers deploy to conflict areas, restoring calm and aiding rebuilding efforts. Their missions stabilize fragile regions, preserving peace and fostering recovery. The army's global reach spans combat zones to research labs. Its forces stand ready at home and abroad, safeguarding national interests.

Meanwhile, scientists and strategists push boundaries, developing advanced technologies and tactics. The army stays vigilant, balancing today's defense with tomorrow's advancements. This approach maintains America's military superiority and anticipates future challenges. For instance, advancements in drone technology and cyber defense are pivotal in modern warfare.

The strong army core values may explain why some soldiers remain at duty stations. After bases close, some recruits stay as ghostly guardians. They symbolize a haunting commitment to put country before self. In the empty halls, the faint echoes of boots on concrete intertwine with whispers of the past, creating an eerie ambiance.

Above left: Posters like this one were placed all over to recruit potential army soldiers. (*James Montgomery Flag*)

Above right: Over 4,000 men and woman gain United States citizenship through joining the United States Army each year. (*Teresa Liu*)

Army men and women all undergo ten weeks of intensive training during boot camp. (*Texas Army ROTC*)

The view from the inside of a U.S. Army Blackhawk helicopter. (*Major Robert Fellingham*)

Above left: Old forts were built with stone walls to protect the soldiers inside. (*Vami IV*)

Above right: Inside the sleeping quarters at a fort, all the essentials were close at hand. (*Vami IV*)

Fort Concho

In 1849, dreamers chased fortunes as gold fever gripped America. It lured colonists across West Texas to California. Army forts dotted the travel routes. They protected settlers seeking riches in the Golden State.

On November 28, 1867, the 4th Cavalry's H Company departed from Fort Chadbourne and went to the Conchos. The 4th Cavalry, known for its vital role in various military campaigns, became a cornerstone of the fort's history.

As the 4th Cavalry's leader touched down, Captain George Huntt named the new fort. Camp Hatch sprang to life, honoring Major John Porter Hatch's leadership. The freshly minted fort stood ready, its christening complete.

This evolution in nomenclature reflects the camp's evolving history and the personnel who served there. In January 1868, Hatch's name changed to Camp Kelly. It honored Captain Michael Kelly, who died of typhoid fever on August 13, 1867. Construction began on Fort Concho north of the camp in March 1868. Over time, the fort served as the base for the 4th and 10th Cavalry. However, the last soldiers marched away, abandoning the fort in June 1889.

Local paranormal teams found a link between hauntings and history when investigating the fort.

Colonel Benjamin Grierson lived in the officer's quarters with his wife Alice and their five children. His thirteen-year-old daughter, Edith, died of typhoid fever on September 9, 1878. Visitors to the fort often glimpse a young girl. Her laughter echoes softly against the cold, stone walls as she plays jacks on the dusty bedroom floor. She pauses only to flash a mischievous smile before darting away. She moves through the officer's lodgings with light and carefree movements. The same girl is seen wearing a peach dress and standing at the top of the staircase.

Graveyard Shift Paranormal Group investigated the fort in 2014. As they entered Emily's room, they heard music playing. The temperature dropped, and the floorboards creaked and groaned. Eager to communicate with their visitor, they left a board game in the room and encouraged Emily to play. Unfortunately, she didn't interact with the game.

The research team also attempted to reach out to Colonel Ranald Mackenzie. Mackenzie earned the nickname "Bad Hand" Mackenzie for losing his fingers in the Civil War and liked to crack the knuckles on his remaining fingers.

Mackenzie died on January 19, 1889. Visitors to the fort report hearing knuckles crack and disembodied voices. A chill raced down the investigators' spines as the temperature plummeted, a tangible reminder that they were not alone in the room.

In Officer Quarters Six, the scent of roses wafts through the air. Visitors glimpse a uniformed figure tending to phantom flowers. Locals believe this is Lieutenant Francis French, Fort Concho's final officer. French's spirit lingers, forever nurturing his beloved blooms.

The final ghost may be Chaplain Dunbar. He appears in the chapel accompanied by a woman believed to be an officer's wife. Lights in the chapel turn off and on, and people hear intangible voices.

Long deserted by the army, this eerie Texas outpost has invisible sentries to repel intruders. Their devotion makes the fort a paranormal hot spot.

Today visitors are welcome to visit Fort Concho and explore the officer's quarters, as well as other buildings. (*Michael Barera*)

The housing on Fort Concho resembles modern military housing. (*Michael Barera*)

Large fields for marching and training surround Fort Concho. (*Michael Barera*)

Enlisted men shared a room with many other soldiers. (*Vami IV*)

The museum opens several buildings for guests to explore. (*Vami IV*)

This is a side view showing the large building with small windows. (*Vami IV*)

The officers' quarters were larger and more domineering than the enlisted quarters. (*Vami IV*)

Visitors can stay the night in certain areas of the fort, but they are warned to watch for unexpected visitors. (*Vami IV*)

Years of Texas weather have battered the sides of many buildings, but they remain standing. (*Vami IV*)

Visible signs of wear are apparent around the windows where boards appear to be falling off the building. (*Vami IV*)

Fort Phantom Hill

During the colonization of Texas, the U.S. Army established a camp on the Clear Fork. The camp was one of many that lined the Texas border to protect migrants passing through the state.

On November 14, 1851, five companies of the 5th Infantry Regiment arrived at the camp. Military records call the site the Post of the Clear Fork of Brazos, but it became known as Fort Phantom Hill.

One legend explains the nickname. The fort stood atop a hill, and the plain's abrupt rise softened with proximity. The height faded, like a mirage, into the distance. Its phantom form dissolved, leaving only a flat expanse.

In August 1853, Colonel William Freeman inspected the fort and found it in poor condition. This prompted orders to abandon the fort on April 6, 1854. Historians think the departing troops likely ignited a blaze that engulfed most of the remaining buildings.

Army troops occupied the fort from 1854 until 1871, serving various military functions. In February 1861, Texas transferred control of the fort to the Confederacy as the Civil War began. This strategic move allowed the Confederacy to strengthen its foothold in the region.

From 1871 to 1875, the fort aided in the transition after Confederate forces surrendered. It became vital in re-establishing federal authority. Its location allowed it to track movements and stabilize the area during Reconstruction.

John Guitar, a civilian, bought the land in 1928 and passed it down to his grandson, Jim Alexander, in 1969. However, not all former occupants understood that the military had closed the facility to operations.

Mona Bell's tragic tale haunts the fort. A soldier's sweetheart, she awaited his return. His headlights flashed three times, signaling her to appear. That fateful night, false rumors of infidelity sparked rage. Blinded by anger, the soldier strangled Mona upon her eager approach. He dumped her body in the frigid waters. Her desperate cries echoed unanswered as she sank beneath the surface. An eerie mist engulfs those who dare flash their lights at the lakeside. Local lore intertwines with the fort's dark history, transforming a once-tender romance into a chilling ghost story that lingers.

During the North Texas Paranormal Society's investigation, they obtained concrete paranormal evidence. On a particularly windy day, the team attempted to collect evidence using a spirit box. Upon review of their recordings, they captured unsettling messages like "God" and "Devil": "A talkative spirit surprised one investigator, who stood over six feet tall, by saying, 'You're tall.'"

The entrance to Fort Phantom Hill looks like the entrance to many of the modern forts today. (*Pi3.124*)

Historic buildings are open for the public to explore but are not as common here as other locations. (*Pi3.124*)

Dirt trails are lined with stone and lead to each of the remaining buildings. (*Pi3.124*)

The green fields make a parklike setting. (*QuesterMark*)

The signage is one of the few remaining signs of the hospital. (*QuesterMark*)

Some of the older structures only have the outside framework remaining. (*QuesterMark*)

The surgeon's office is marked with a sign. (*QuesterMark*)

Historical markers tell the story of the Fort Phantom Hill and its life over the years. (*Pi3.124*)

5
Coast Guard

Founded in 1790, the U.S. Coast Guard is a unique military branch. During peacetime, it falls under the command of the Department of Homeland Security. However, during wartime, it transfers to the Department of Defense.

The government formed the coast guard to protect American commerce from smuggling and piracy. Its mission has since expanded greatly.

The coast guard coordinates with the navy to ensure defense readiness. Port and waterway security remains a top priority. Maritime law enforcement effectively combats drug and human trafficking and illegal immigration.

Their mission evolved from manning lighthouses to maintaining them. In 1998, Boston Light's last keeper retired, ending an era of keepers. Now, coast guard crews service these historic beacons, preserving their legacy. This shift showcases technological progress but also a bittersweet change in maritime culture. As the coast guard's role has evolved, so too have the lighthouses that stand as sentinels along our coasts, each with its own story of service and sacrifice.

Like the navy, the U.S. Coast Guard is a protector of the waterways and the vessels which travel those waterways. (*Petty Officer 3rd Class Paige Hause*)

Sometimes the water is rough, or the climate is cold, which means the coast guard must dress for the occasion. (*Petty Officer 3rd Class Jennifer Nease*)

Some of the larger coast guard boats resemble large pirate ships with mighty, powerful sails. (*Petty Officer 2nd Class Patrick Kelley*)

Like all other branches of the military, the coast guard is always training. Here sailors are seen perched on the top of the sails. (*Petty Officer 2nd Class Patrick Kelley*)

Sabine Pass Lighthouse and Coast Guard Station #216

A beacon, funded by Congress a decade earlier, rose at the Sabine River's mouth in 1857. This first-class lighthouse guided sailors to shore without incident.

Nearby, a lifeboat station emerged in 1879, boosting local maritime protection. In 1904, flames devoured the station. The coast guard rebuilt the base. For generations, it was a steadfast guardian, keeping seafarers safe along the treacherous coastline.

The Sabine Lighthouse became entangled in Civil War turmoil. In 1861, Confederate forces doused its guiding flame, hoping to impede Union vessels with a blanket of darkness. The weathered lighthouse loomed against the smoky horizon, witnessing the chaos below. Two battles etched violent chapters into its history.

The first battle took place on September 25, 1862. The Union sought to capture the Confederate forts at Sabine Pass and control the Texas coast. The skirmish was brief but intense, marked by sharp exchanges of gunfire. After just a few hours of fighting, the Union forces, surprised by the strong resistance, pulled back to save their strength for later battles.

The second battle took place on September 8, 1863. The Union entered Sabine Pass and immediately came under fire from the Confederates. As cannons roared, Confederate forces struck hard at Union gunboats. Two vessels fell silent. Bullets flew, and soldiers fell.

Ultimately, the Union suffered over 200 casualties, including dead, injured, and captured men. When the smoke cleared, Southern flags waved with great fanfare. Victory belonged to the Confederacy in this fierce clash of arms.

During World War II, the coast guard station suffered two casualties in the line of duty. It highlighted the dangers of serving in the coast guard. On March 27, 1943, Patrolman Charles Alford was on a routine beach patrol. His horse reared without warning, flinging the patrolman through the air. He died from a skull fracture. On December 9, 1943, SN1 Royal Legendre drowned when he fell overboard from the station's patrol boat.

The once-bustling tower now stands alone, its guiding light extinguished in 1952. After the lighthouse fulfilled its duties, supernatural tales began to take root. They wove a rich tapestry of local lore that persists.

On misty evenings at Sabine Pass, spectral booms echo through the silence. A phantom Confederate ship appears, its silhouette flickering like a candle in the fog. This evokes a haunting nostalgia for the battles that once raged nearby.

Perhaps the hurricane haunted the lighthouse if not the battle. The 1886 hurricane relentlessly battered the lighthouse. Keeper Gustave Hummeland, Henry Plummer and his wife, and Clara Marty sought shelter inside. As winds intensified, they climbed to the tower's peak. Gustave struggled to hold down the massive trapdoor, using his body and a heavy oil can for weight. For two days, they huddled together against the biting cold, their stomachs gnawing with hunger as the storm raged outside.

Some say Gustave, Henry, and Clara still linger, ghostly companions watching over the lighthouse. Their voices and footsteps remain and often frighten visitors.

Dress for visitors, the docked vessel welcomes public tours. (*United States Coast Guard*)

Water rescue can require the use of helicopters to assist in the safe recovery of victims. (*Petty Officer 1st Class Andrew Kendrick*)

The top section of the lighthouse has been relocated. (*Patrick Feller*)

There is a historical site at the location of the battleground in Sabine. (*Patrick Feller*)

The park at the historical site for the battleground. (*Patrick Feller*)

The lighthouse at Sabine Pass. (*Patrick Feller*)

This antique postcard was published by Thomas Wilson. (*Don Kelly Southeast Texas Postcard Collection*)

Today the lighthouse is nearly hidden with vegetation. (*Matthew White*)

A monument at the Sabine Pass Lighthouse. (*P13.124*)

A coast guard cutter off the coast of Texas. (*Petty Officer 2nd Class Patrick Kelley*)

Point (Port) Isabel Lighthouse

On September 28, 1850, Congress allocated $15,000 to build a lighthouse at Brazos Santiago Pass. Work started two years later, and when finished, the lighthouse stood 82 feet tall. The brick tower started with four lights and was then upgraded to fifteen lights and twenty-one reflectors.

In 1857, officials added a groundbreaking invention: the Fresnel lens. This lens produced a brighter, more focused beam of light, greatly improving visibility for passing ships.

Like many lighthouses, it also housed soldiers during the Civil War. Both Union and Confederate soldiers used the site as a lookout post. After the war, it returned to operation in 1866 and stayed lit until a land dispute in 1888. Locals stated that the government did not have a title for the land on which the lighthouse stood.

The government turned off the light in 1905 and sold the lighthouse on September 20, 1927. A local citizen bought the lighthouse and its property. Restoration work started in 1951, and the site opened to the public in 1952.

On stormy nights, locals claim to see a shadowy figure cloaked in mist hovering near the top of the lighthouse. Sailors claim it is a guardian angel helping to guide the ships as the lighthouse did in its day.

Another tale is about the haunting of the seventeenth step.

"We bet you can't stand on step seventeen for seventeen minutes," a taunting friend challenged a brave young man.

The man accepted the challenge without hesitation. The clock ticked as he embarked on this unusual test of patience and stamina. Friends could only watch as he experienced a sudden and fatal accident. Some say he fell, but others believe an invisible force pushed him.

At the seventeenth step, visitors report a sense of unease, and some hear whispers in their ears as a cold breeze brushes past them.

Several paranormal groups have investigated the lighthouse and keeper's cottage. They have found cold spots, heard voices and footsteps, and seen shadow figures. Investigators also reported feeling that someone touched them and said mysterious lights illuminated the area.

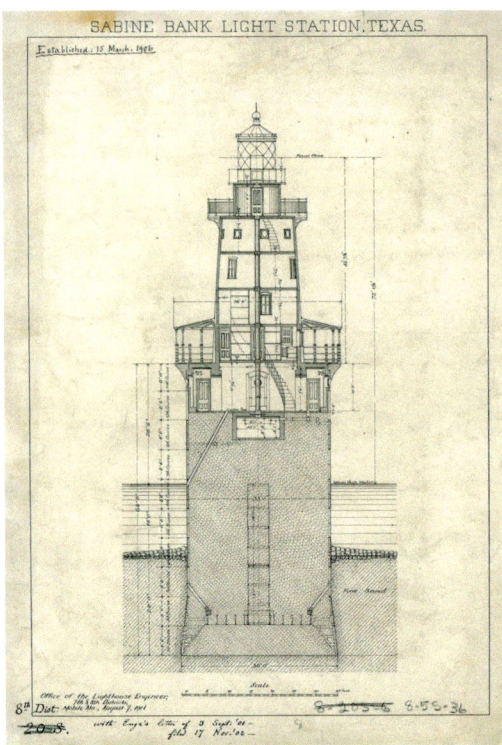

Left: The blueprint for Sabine Lighthouse. (*Public Domain*)

Below: The keeper's house of a local coast guard station is often nearby a lighthouse to help with maintenance. (*Petty Officer 2nd Class Nathan Henise*)

Coast Guard

Right: From this angle there is a small window near the top of the lighthouse. (*Carol M. Highsmith*)

Below: The stark white tower of the Port Isabel lighthouse is bright against a blue sky. (*Billy D. Wagner*)

Above left: This photo from 2011 shows the entrance to the lighthouse and trailing leading up to the entrance. (*Carol M. Highsmith*)

Above right: This historical black and white image shows the view of the inside of the lighthouse. (*Bartlett Cocke*)

Left: This historical black and white photo shows the very top of the lighthouse, from the inside. (*Bartlett Cocke*)

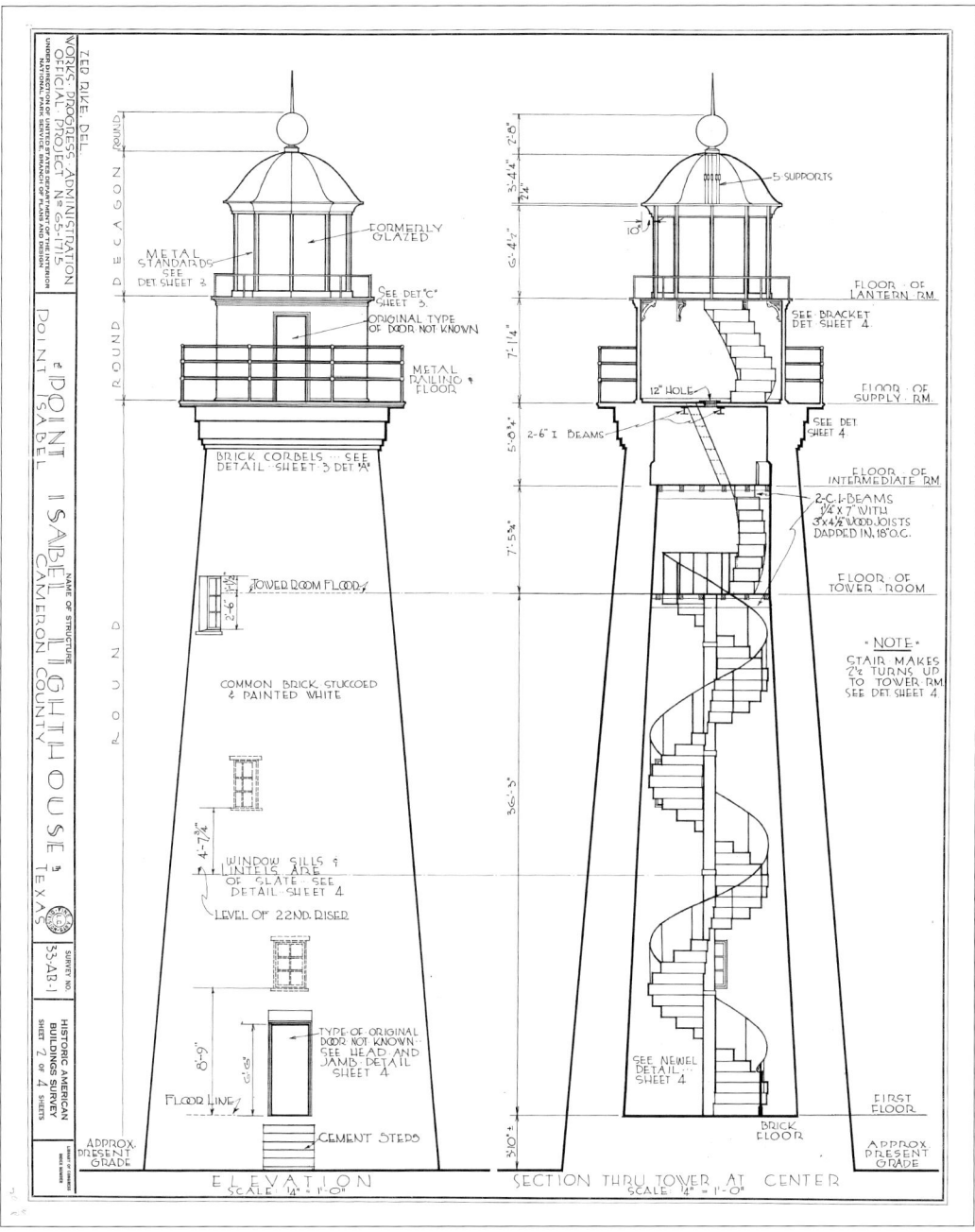

The blueprint image of the Point Isabel lighthouse shows the winding stairs to the top. (*Public Domain*)

6
Air Force

On August 1, 1907, the U.S. Army Signal Corps established an aeronautical division to handle U.S. air and space superiority. The division would control airspace, allowing U.S. forces free movement and limiting enemies. It would train for rapid global strike capabilities and provide rapid mobility of troops, equipment, and supplies. The division was also tasked with gathering and analyzing intelligence for U.S. military operations.

The U.S. Air Force has three central values: Integrity First, Service Before Self, and Excellence in All We Do. They believe members should be accountable, honest and do what is right, even when no one is watching. Selfless dedication drives their pursuit of excellence. Relentlessly refining their craft, they strive to exceed hopes and elevate others. Generous passion fuels their quest for mastery. Their drive to improve lives sets high standards and fuels growth.

This drawing shows what the area around the lighthouse looked like when it was first built. (C. E. H. Bonwill)

This early drawing of the lighthouse shows what it looked like when it was first constructed. (Public Domain)

Above left: This image of the exterior is from 2001 and shows years of weather aging. (*Bartlett Cocke*)

Above right: The paved trail up to the lighthouse is lined with white stone. (*Billy D. Wagner*)

Bergstrom Air Force Base

On the evening of December 29, 1980, Betty Cash drove her car down a road near Dayton, Texas. Vickie Landrum sat in the passenger seat, and her grandson, Colby, was in the back seat. It was getting late as they drove down the isolated two-lane highway.

The women noticed a bright light above the trees. Given the proximity of Houston International Airport and Bergstrom Air Force Base, such lights were not unusual.

A few minutes passed, and the light began to grow brighter. As the light intensified, the car's interior grew uncomfortably hot, so Betty decided to stop and investigate.

After pulling to the side of the narrow road, both women exited the car. Betty and Vickie spotted a bright, silver, diamond-shaped object as big as the town water tower. Small blue lights flashed around the center, and flames shot out of the bottom.

The heat radiated like a furnace, forcing Betty to shield her skin with her jacket as her heart raced with fear and curiosity. The woman returned to the safety of the car. With her hand on the dashboard, Betty left an imprint as the plastic began to melt under the heat.

A group of military helicopters filled the sky and surrounded the mysterious object. With this, the object rose in elevation and disappeared.

After this strange encounter, all three occupants of the vehicle became ill. They exhibited nausea, vomiting, diarrhea, general weakness, and a burning sensation in their eyes. Betty, who stayed out of the car the longest, suffered the most.

The U.S. Air Force is known for its mighty fighter jets. (*Don Ramey Logan*)

This image shows a fighter jet in flight over the clouds and mountain terrain. (*Senior Airman Brett Clashman*)

U.S. Air Force fighter pilots must undergo years of intensive training and be able to perform unthinkable feats in the air. (*David Armer*)

Air force men and women stand in rows on the tarmac. (*Alan Quevy*)

Air Force

Eight months after the incident, interviews occurred at the air force base. They denied the presence of military helicopters on the night in question.

In the end, *Texas Monthly* stated, "To this day, there is no conclusive explanation for the night's events."

Betty's symptoms grew more mysterious. Painful skin blisters emerged, and her hair started falling out. For fifteen days, baffled physicians pondered her case. At last, they cracked the medical mystery: radiation sickness. Each ailment compounded her suffering, challenging her strength and resilience throughout her life. In 1983, doctors diagnosed Betty with breast cancer. The only explanation for the radiation exposure was the mysterious glowing object.

In the 1950s and 1960s, several reports of unidentified flying objects near Bergstrom surfaced. Witnesses reported strange lights and objects moving at a high rate of speed. Bright lights and disc-shaped objects astounded observers in the 1970s. Their impossible maneuvers defied known technology, mystifying both military and civilian witnesses. Reports intensified near the base in the following decade. Triangular craft and eerie light formations emerged as new phenomena. These silent, enigmatic objects drifted across the sky, leaving witnesses in awe.

Locals in the area today wonder about the connections between the air force and the UFO sightings.

Not all air force planes are used for military battles. (*Staff Sargent Nicholas Larsen*)

The up-close view of this plane shows the size of the engine. (*Airman 1st Class Eve Daugherty*)

Bergstrom Air Force Base once held countless planes and the hustle and bustle of a popping military base. (*CMSgt. Don C. Sutherland*)

Right: This artist's drawing shows what may have occurred on that night when a UFO made a visit to Bergstrom. (*Cindi Tune*)

Below: The air base saw many visitors over the years, including the queen of England. (*Jerry Wilson*)

The U.S. president travels in style with the *Air Force One* jet. (*Airman 1st Class Jason P. Robertson*)

Pyote Air Force Base

In 1942, Pyote Air Force Base opened to train B-17 Flying Fortress crews during World War II. The rattlesnakes on the tarmacs inspired a unique nickname: Rattlesnake Bomber Base. It reflected these unexpected runway invaders.

During World War II, Pyote became the most extensive bomber base in the country. Skilled bomber pilots emerged through intense training, which, while effective, often proved fatal. Frequent casualties marked the path from novice to expert.

On June 23, 1943, an unnamed individual loaded a bomb onto a B-17 Flying Fortress. This act resulted in a devastating explosion that triggered a chain reaction of secondary blasts. The catastrophic event claimed the lives of twenty-three soldiers and one civilian, leaving the base in shock and mourning. Investigators later found that an unsecured bomb caused the deadly incident. In the wake of this devastating loss, the military recognized the urgent need for enhanced safety measures.

After the war, Pyote shifted from a training ground to a storage facility. In 1948, it housed over 2,000 abandoned military planes. A mosaic of aircraft blanketed the airfield. Massive B-29s dwarfed the reliable B-17s, while nimble B-25s and A-26s wove between them. The patchwork of bombers formed a living, breathing quilt of military might across the tarmac.

Above: Air force planes flying side by side over the land below. (*TSgt. Michael Haggerty*)

Right: Lt. Gen. Charles J. Cunningham Jr. led Bergstrom command. (*Public Domain*)

Lone Star Shadows

Parachutes are released to slow down the speed of a fighter jet as it lands. (*TSgt Lou Hernandez*)

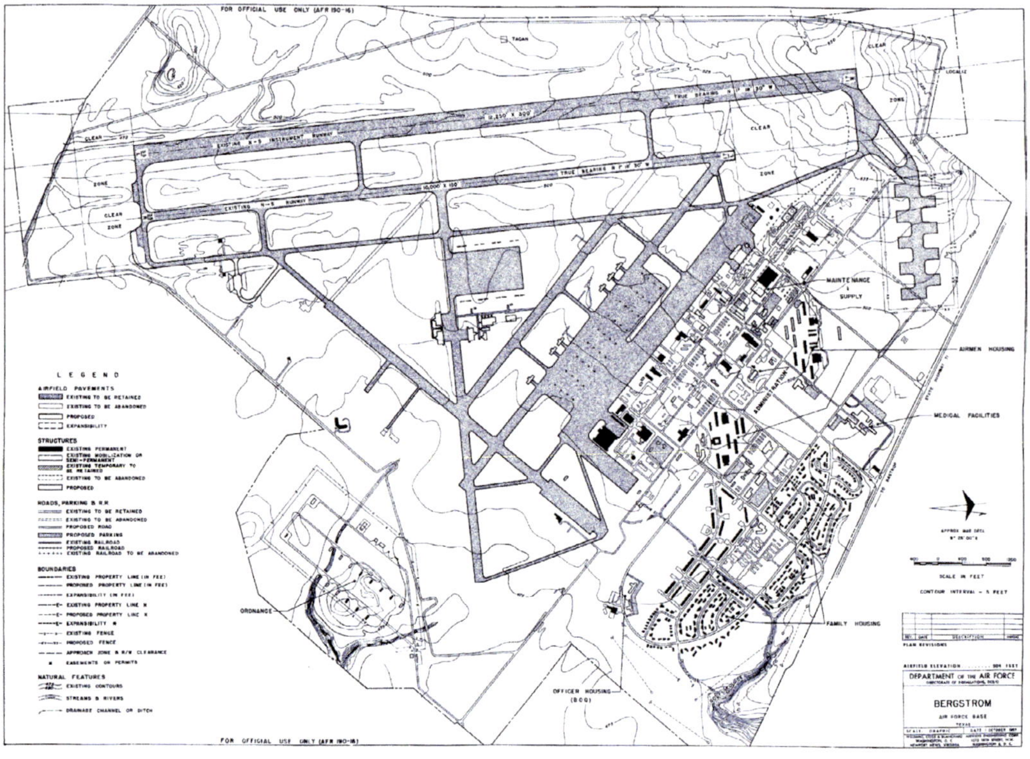

Blueprint drawing of the Bergstrom Air Force Base. (*Department of Defense*)

On July 3, 1949, the *Enola Gay* touched down at Pyote, destined for temporary storage. This remarkable bomber stood out among the abandoned fleet. Its weathered fuselage and battle scars told a story of resilience and destruction, drawing the eyes of all who passed by. The *Enola Gay* earned every dent and scratch as it made its mark in history.

Colonel Paul Tibbets, piloting the historic aircraft, chose "Enola Gay" as its moniker. This tribute to his mother changed a private gesture into a lasting symbol of World War II's most divisive mission. *Enola Gay* was one of the first B-29s modified to carry nuclear weapons.

Tibbets took off from the Tinian Islands on August 6, 1945, holding a uranium bomb known as Little Boy. As Hiroshima's skyline crumbled, a single bomb erased three-quarters of the city.

On another mission, Nagasaki suffered atomic devastation. The *Enola Gay*, already infamous for its role in Hiroshima, struck its target once more. This B-29 bomber had the distinction of witnessing history twice.

Enola Gay's silent vigil at Pyote lasted over four years post-retirement. Then, on December 2, 1953, the bomber soared to Andrews Air Force Base. Skilled hands began preservation work. Its last stop: the Smithsonian. A powerful reminder of its world-altering role in history.

Another famous plane visited Pyote. Half swan and half goose, the *Swoose* departed in December 1953. The mighty Boeing B-17 Flying Fortress saw extensive use in World War II and became the oldest intact B-17. It is the only known "shark fin" tailed B-17. Withdrawn from duty in March 1942, the *Swoose* was in poor condition from countless flight hours. It is currently in a restoration process.

At the start of 1950, the demand for B-29 bombers surged. The Korean War required refurbishing these aircraft for active-duty units in combat. During the battle, the U.S. military recognized the need for jets to keep up with the Soviet MiG-15s. The propeller-driven bombers stored at Pyote became obsolete. Salvage operations began as Pyote shifted toward recycling components and metals.

The air force scheduled the base for deactivation on December 31, 1953. Although abandoned, most of the permanent buildings and hangars remain.

Operations at Pyote ceased on August 1, 1963. As the last echoes of aircraft faded, rattlesnakes reclaimed the land.

The entrance to Rattlesnake Bomber Base. (*Surely Shirly*)

Another angle of the entrance to the base. (*Nicolas Henderson*)

A historical marker indicates the former base. (*Nicholas Henderson*)

The *Enola Gay* is now on display for visitors to admire. (*Bernt Rostad*)

Up-close view of an F-16 fighter jet. (*Staff Sgt. Cherie A. Thurby*)

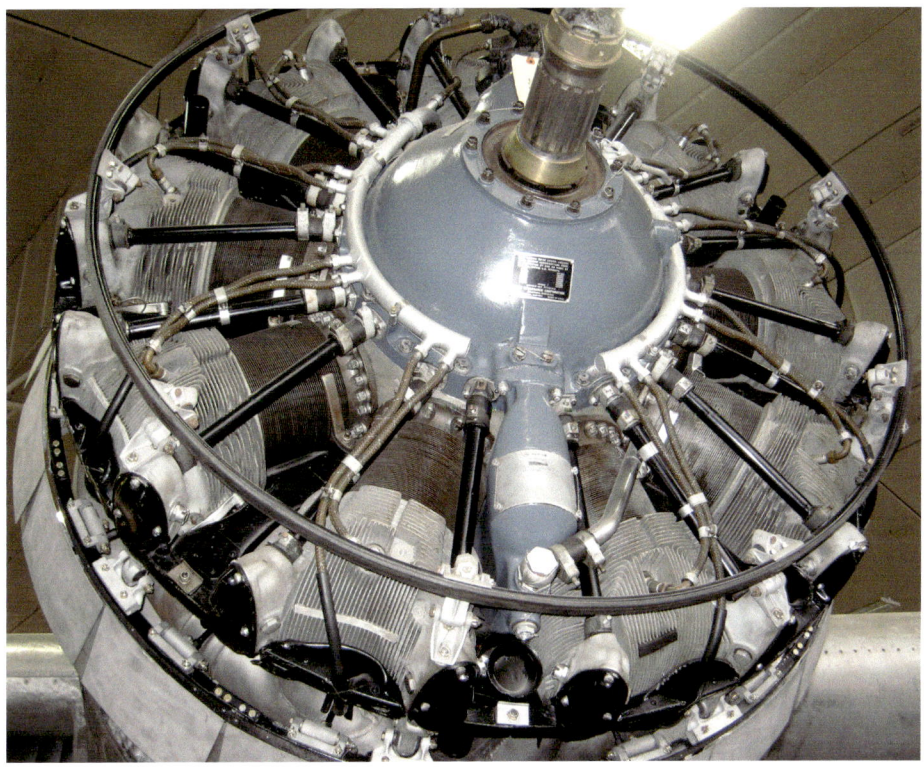

The engine of the Boeing B-17 Flying Fortress *Swoose*. (*Mark Jones Jr.*)

The uniform logo for the space force. (*U.S. Space & Missile Defense Command*)

Twelve new astronaut candidates at Johnson Space Center in Houston, Texas. (*NASA Johnson*)

The abandoned Saturn V Apollo rocket at Johnson Space Center. (*Tim Pearce*)

7

Space Force

U.S. Air Force, Army, and Navy space programs date back to the beginning of the Cold War. Combining ideas from each branch, the air force established the U.S. Space Force on December 20, 2019.

General Henry "Hap" Arnold was a five-star general in the air force. He was one of the first military pilots, and Orville and Wilbur Wright trained him. During his forty-two-year career, Arnold's intelligence helped boost the U.S. in air science. Recognizing the critical role space would play in future military operations, he influenced the development of jet planes, rocketry, and supersonic flight.

Arnold's pioneering contributions in aviation and rocketry propelled the air force to take the lead in military space initiatives and set up its first space unit in 1954.

In 1961, the air force seized control of military space operations. Cosmic defense evolved as the Pentagon launched its audacious space initiative. This space strategy secured military dominance, changed warfare, and marked a shift in global security.

Born from necessity, the space force safeguards America's celestial frontier, monitoring potential threats. It enables movement through space, conducts defense operations, and ensures stability in space activities. Working with allies, it provides satellite access, missile warnings, and navigation systems. These vigilant sky-scanners decode cosmic clues, tracking earthly foes and potential hostile visitors. The space force protects America's interests in this uncharted territory as nations play interstellar chess.

There are no space force bases in Texas. However, Texas is a vital hub for military training and space operations. Lackland Air Force Base trains air force and space force recruits.

A few monumental rockets and space artifacts now call Houston, Texas, home. Officials preserved them in museums after they faced abandonment and brought pieces of abandoned space close to home. These historical artifacts reside at the Johnson Space Center. They are educational tools to bridge the gap between past space exploration and the space force's future.

The abandoned space shuttle *Independence*. (*Reinhard Link*)

The tail section of the Saturn V rocket. (*Wally Gobetz*)

Abandoned rockets adorn the grassy area outside of the Johnson Space Center. (*Wally Gobetz*)

Parts of abandoned spacecraft are displayed all over the space center. (*Wally Gobetz*)

Presentation of the U.S. Space Force flag. (*The White House*)